Speak

BRITTAINY SPENCER

13TH & JOAN

For permission requests, write to the publisher, addressed "Attention: Permissions Coordinator," 205 N. Michigan Avenue, Suite #810, Chicago, IL 60601. 13th & Joan books may be purchased for educational, business or sales promotional use. For information, please email the Sales Department at sales@13thandjoan.com.

Printed in the U. S. A.

First Printing, November 2023.

Library of Congress Cataloging-in-Publication Data has been applied for.

ISBN: 978-1-961863-22-4

DEDICATION

This book is dedicated to my Aunt Debra Mauldin. You taught me to never let anyone take my power. Every time I recite those words I hear your voice, I see your face, and I'm reminded of my inner strength. Thank you for being one of the strongest women in my life. I love you and I miss you. Consider this book Volume I of me taking my power back.

DEAR READER

KNOW WHAT IT feels like to have your power taken away from you. What should have always been in your hands was now in someone else's back pocket. My Aunt Debra used to tell me, "Never let anyone take your power." Every time I repeat those words from her in my mind or aloud, I'm reminded that my strength and my power belong to me and I am in control of my life. There's been a lot of shit I've encountered along the way. During *this* journey, you'll be immersed in my personal experiences as a child, woman, and mother who has suffered from abandonment, bullying, sexual abuse, sexual harassment, and rape. I'm still here, still standing. I wasn't always strong enough to tell my story but today, my storytelling begins.

I have spent the past few years reconnecting with the power that I thought had been stolen. In this book I share the loss of that power with you, but I also share how I learned to use my voice to get my power back. Like you, I'm stuck riding this roller coaster we call life when I'd much rather prefer a slower-paced ride, like a carousel or Ferris wheel. But life is funny that way. Things happen that are out of our control, situations that rob us of our personal power. Not me, not anymore.

Brittainy Spencer

ACKNOWLEDGEMENTS

KATELYN, year after year you have encouraged me to write a book. Your support has been monumental in this process. Thank you for being an amazingly supportive friend over the last 20 years and for pushing me to do what has always been in my heart.

TIFFANY, thank you for helping me align my thoughts and ideas, for always encouraging me, and for your never-ending love and support.

MOMMY, I know this was tough for you. Thank you for helping me with the timeline and for understanding that this is life through my eyes. This is not a reflection of you or your parenting, but it's important for me to acknowledge the cause and effect of certain decisions and actions. This is part of my journey.

To my first career coach, COURTNEY BALL, you changed my life. You read one of the very first stories in this book two years before publishing. You continue to support and encourage me. My love and respect for you run deep. You helped me reach my goals and so much more. Thank you.

QUA, without you introducing me to this publisher via Instagram many moons ago, I would not have come so far in this process this quickly. It was your book, *Self-love, A Silent Revolution*, that truly inspired me. You showed me I could do it. I could put everything down on paper–the good, the bad, the joy, the pain, the trauma, the love–and turn that into growth and fearlessness. Thank you for being my guiding light.

Lastly, my therapist, TINA! Each week you help me believe in myself a little bit more, grow a little bit more, and become comfortable with being uncomfortable. Thank you for watering me.

Some names and identifying details have been changed to protect the privacy of individuals. For those who know me personally, you may recognize aspects of the story and the people in it. The stories in this book are my recollection of life-altering events that I eagerly share, with one sole purpose: To tell the truth.

Content Warning: This memoir contains sensitive and at times graphic content related to rape, sex, and trauma. It is possible you may experience some discomfort or emotional disturbance while reading.

TABLE OF CONTENTS

INTRODUCTION

T HE PURPOSE OF this memoir is to tell the truth. I've endured a lot, and I've never truly spoken up or out for fear of being misunderstood, for fear of not being believed. Now, I owe it to myself and the people in my life to allow my story to be heard in the hope that maybe I might help or impact someone who is afraid to use their voice, afraid to speak up, or protect themselves. It has taken me a long time to learn the power of the word "NO" and to gain back control of my own body and truly believe in myself. In speaking our truth, we find the power and courage to overcome fear, be brave, and display acts of self-love publicly. We learn to let go of emotions that no longer serve our being.

I've been confused. I've been hurt, and I've hurt others. I've cried endlessly. I've felt lost, hopeless, and empty. I've been angry. I've been sad. I've been embarrassed and ashamed. I've been infuriated. I've been scared and fearful. I've felt alone and abandoned. I've been unsure of myself and insecure. I've suffered, but I've also learned. In the midst of pain buried deep down, I've still managed to succeed in my own way. I'm here, within these pages, blooming before my own eyes.

When I look at my life and some of the things I've experienced, I realize the only place to go from here is UP. Here I am within these pages bearing my soul and asking you to rise up with me. Rise up against peer pressure, bullying, sexual harassment, rape, fake-ass friends, and people who would rather see you fall than lift you up. I no longer hold space for that.

At the end of each chapter, you'll find questions or the option to journal to help you reflect on your own experiences. You may be asking yourself, *"Why do I need to reflect? What is the purpose or importance of this?"* Taking a moment to give thought to a situation or scenario provides each of us with the opportunity to dive deeper and consider *"What does this mean for me? What did I learn? Did I learn anything at all?"* For some of us, setting aside time to reflect could mean taking our power back. For others, it can be the opportunity to start their own healing journey.

In my experience with practicing reflection, I've learned that there is power in pondering. Reflection can allow you to have a greater understanding of who you are and how you operate; your abilities, strengths, and values. Reflection can help you strengthen your relationship with yourself, and it can also be a difficult or uncomfortable experience.

The goal is to be honest with yourself and to learn or unlearn ways of being and doing.

This book is just as much about YOU as it is me. I'm not the only human to experience what's beyond this page. With all we face everyday we're still here.

To those still finding your voice, do not give up. Your voice is your most powerful weapon. Use it.

P.S. Dear POC (People of Color): Therapy is not just for white people. You can attend church *and* see a therapist. I know for many of us, God, Jesus, and spirituality are naturally our first line of defense. I'm here to tell you, there is no harm in having a second line of defense for your well-being. It is okay to not be okay and talk to a professional. Whether that be a therapist or counselor, you have the option and you are capable of making good decisions for yourself. In my personal experiences with therapy, I've had better results with a mental health professional who looks like me, but to each their own.

CHAPTER I:
THERE'S NO PLACE LIKE HOME

I DIDN'T UNDERSTAND WHY we were leaving so early in the morning, but Mom hurriedly loaded up her 1995 two-door green Mitsubishi Eclipse with as much of our clothes, toys, shoes, and other belongings stuffed into suitcases, plastic bins, and garbage bags. The trunk was packed to the brim, our things spilling over into the backseat like the leaves of an overgrown bush.

My sister Jasmine and I, oblivious to what was actually happening at the tender ages of 6 and 8, were swept up in what I now know to be our parents' drama. We were awakened from our sleep and rushed outside and into the car. I remember our matching floral nightgowns, white and speckled with daisies, and the warmth of the sun against my face. We both clung to our favorite dolls and followed the lead of our mother like typical baby ducklings, staying close to her side.

I can still see my father's face in the screen door of our home as we backed out of the driveway, looking on helplessly. In that moment, it was as if I could see his heart drop out of his chest and onto the ground. At that time in my life, I'd never seen my father look so sad. Yet I never really understood the pain he must've felt until now. The despair and the fear of the unknown for your children are some of the most gut-wrenching feelings you can ever experience. You start to imagine every dangerous scenario simply because you don't know if your child is safe and have no control over the situation. As the mother of an 11-year-old beautiful boy who has experienced the pain of not knowing where your child is at the hands of the other parent, I now understand every ounce of his pain.

It would be at least 730 days before we saw our father's face again.

We left that morning and embarked on a 19-hour drive from East Hartford, Connecticut, to Birmingham, Alabama. Far as fuck. While writing this memoir, I googled and mapped the route from our childhood home in Connecticut to Charles A. Brown Elementary, the first school we attended in Birmingham. It is a 16-hour drive from the home my dad still lives in today, and we only stopped once before arriving at our final destination.

Our stop in Tennessee is one of the very few things I remember about that trip. It may have been because we finally stopped driving or because we stayed in a hotel. But I think I remember Tennessee because of the breathtaking

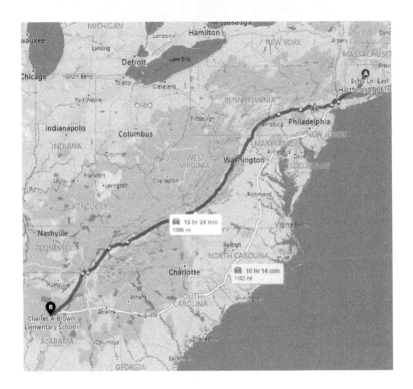

beauty of the Appalachian Mountains that span from Quebec to Northern Alabama.

The Great Smoky Mountains are a sub-range that lies between Tennessee and North Carolina, and we drove right into them. The mountains were unimaginably large and vast for my little 8-year-old mind. The trees seemed to stretch endlessly for miles, covering the massive mountain tops. The air around the mountains was foggy, cloudy, and absolutely beautiful. The land looked perfectly untouched. I'd never seen grass so green or trees so large, mountainscapes that spanned beyond my line of sight. Decades later I haven't forgotten that feeling of complete awe in the presence of nature.

Why did my mom choose to drive us all the way to Alabama? Well, my mom was born in Connecticut but spent her childhood in Selma, Alabama, where her mother's family is from. Our extended family is sprinkled all over the South. Mom's side is native to Bama and dad's side is native to the Carolinas.

We also had plenty of family in Connecticut. Mom's entire immediate family resided within a 10-mile radius of our home in East Hartford and my dad's sister Charlene lived right next door to us, but I guess at the time my mom had already made up her mind that leaving for Alabama was the best decision for all of us. We were completely unprepared for what for me was life-altering and ultimately some of the most damaging years of my life–and that's just the half of it.

The move to Alabama was the first time my family was separated but it wouldn't be the last. From the age of 8 until about 14, I attended nine different schools between Connecticut and Alabama. In the fourth grade alone, I attended two elementary schools. That was the year my struggles with math began. Sure, lots of people dislike math, but the way my mind couldn't grasp it to this day astonishes me. The numbers just seemed to jump around and dance on the page, like the famous Keith Haring Mural.

I haven't quite yet figured out the correlation between my disdain for math and the course of my life, but I'm certain it's all related. In fourth grade, *when I was in school,* basic algebra was introduced. In algebra there are unknown variables, factors to solve for, and numbers that equal letters. It never made any sense to me. It felt like a foreign land that I did not have the strength to conquer or understand. I was already in a strange new world. I didn't have the mental capacity for equations. I continued to struggle with math right into college, only barely passing every single year and never getting anything higher than a C. My other grades kept me afloat.

In our new school, Brown Elementary, we wore uniforms. We never had to wear uniforms before. My sister and I didn't sound like the other kids or even act like them. Our accents were strange but so were theirs. Everyone everywhere was Black, which was exciting and also very different. In class, there were mainly Black students and more Black teachers than I had ever seen. Schools back home were a lot more diverse. My best friend in Connecticut was named Jenny and she was Laotian. Our next-door neighbor was a hearing-disabled white woman who was incredibly kind and had a beautiful garden. The kids and people in our neighborhood were white, Black, Puerto Rican, or mixed race.

Our world before and the new world we were immersed in looked and felt like polar opposites. We left our three-bedroom, 1.5-bath duplex in a quiet cul-de-sac and moved in with our cousin Jean and her two kids,Cameron and Shanti. My mom, sister, and I shared a room. The homes in the two states aren't even built the same. In New England, you typically see colonial and Cape Cod-style homes with basements. In Birmingham, a lot of the homes are ranches or bungalows without basements. The weather, as you can imagine, is extremely different. Alabama's heat was both ferocious and sweltering. There was also the new danger of tornadoes. It was all *so* different.

I have a love-hate relationship with Alabama. It's where my love of the show *King of the Hill* grew, where I saw my first Black marching band, and where I met my Big Sister Virginia Bowman from the Big Brother Big Sister Program. Alabama is where I first remember experiencing racism, where I had my first kiss and lost my first elementary school fight. It's where I experienced a lot of bullying from both family and so-called friends. It's where I experienced the height of my childhood sexual harassment and became rebellious and somewhat violent toward my sister because I felt no one could be trusted, not even those closest to you. I learned a lot in Alabama, probably a little too much.

I don't think anything was more shocking, scary, or confusing than the few months our family spent at the homeless shelter. Cousin Jean either kicked my mom out or we left. Either way we were abruptly uprooted yet again but this time, we arrived at a women's homeless shelter. We shared a room with a white woman and her younger daughter Shelby who was around 6 years old. The three of us often played together and slept together. Shelby and her mom were like family up until they left a few months later.

The room we lived in had concrete walls and a cafeteria-style tile floor, if you can call that a style. There were three wood frame bunk beds along each of the walls and on the fourth wall was the door to the shared bathroom. The time at the homeless shelter was very confusing and if I'm being honest, my brain has done away with most of it. I've only held on to what was really good or really bad. Everything in between is a blur.

I remembered our new school and feeling awfully worried about my sister in second grade. I was constantly worried. There was always a new face and unfamiliar terrain. My mom made sure we were okay but our constant transitions hardly ever came with an explanation or the truth. At least at the shelter, we got to celebrate Christmas.

My mom was raised as a Jehovah's Witness and she raised my sister and me that way *sometimes*, meaning we didn't celebrate holidays often. It happened occasionally and when it did, it was always THE BOMB. (I'm aging myself, but it's the most accurate description for a kid who grew up in the late 1990s and early 2000s). As crazy as it sounds, Christmas at the homeless shelter was one of the highlights of my childhood. My sister and I left our family dorm and walked down to the cafeteria that was decorated with colorful Christmas lights, garlands, and a big beautiful ornate tree. We were greeted by Santa, and he excitedly handed us one big black garbage bag each FULL of toys. There were so many things to play with and so much to be grateful for. We happily dragged our bags back to our room and spent the day playing with and exploring our new presents! Thankfully, my mom kept us in one spot for the remainder of the school year. By the summer of 1997, we were moving into a new apartment and enrolled to attend another school. My little sister was entering third grade and I was entering fifth.

REALITY CHECK:

Childhood trauma is real and occurs more than you'd think. According to the Substance Abuse and Mental Health Administration, at least two-thirds of children report at least one traumatic event by age 16. Trauma comes in many forms. It could be the loss of a parent, witnessing domestic or community violence, a natural disaster, or even moving around a lot. By the time I reached fifth grade, I experienced numerous traumatic events. Needless to say, the impact of that trauma led me to struggle in many areas throughout my life. I suffered from PTSD, a lack of impulse control, low self-esteem, depression, anxiety, and anger issues–to name a few. I didn't overcome many of these issues until adulthood. I held everything in and I didn't talk about it. Yet, I was still able to function daily, which led me to believe that to some extent I was okay.

I believed I'd somehow outsmarted my demons. I was wrong. My demons silently followed me and showed up later in life. For many years I struggled with communication, specifically in relationships and self-love. Writing and therapy helped me to heal those wounds from childhood and made my emotional load easier to bear.

We all have things from our past or childhood that haunt or impact us in different ways. I want to remind you that you don't have to carry that pain with you every day. Write it out, talk to a professional, and speak your truth. Some say, *"The truth will set you free"* and for me, speaking my truth has allowed me to let go of my fears and of the pain I carried for so long.

If there is something you feel compelled to express, something from your childhood that still impacts or hurts you, I've included space on the next page to write it down if you feel comfortable doing so. This is your chance to release and practice letting go.

Let it go...

_____

_____

_____

_____

_____

_____

_____

Speak

_____

_____

_____

_____

_____

_____

_____

_____

_____

_____

_____

_____

_____

CHAPTER II:
LOST GIRL

I'M NOT SURE what was worse, fifth grade or middle school. Either way, fifth grade was a very angry, aggressive, and somewhat exploratory period of my life. It's when weekly neighborhood fights became part of my norm. Jasmine and I were picked on constantly because of our differences. Our Northern accents, different ways of doing things, even our clothes. Mom always dressed us to the nines. Although we wore uniforms at school like everyone else, every inch of our uniforms was Tommy Hilfiger. In the 90s, Tommy Hilfiger was hot shit and the logo on our pants and shirts made us a target for kids at school. We stood out.

Bullying seemed to follow us to every school, and I've attended nearly a dozen. The bullying I experienced in middle school was nothing like the petty shit in elementary school, like the time Jasmine came home with her shirt covered in chocolate milk because one of her classmates poured it on her at lunch. Or the time she attempted to walk back to her desk and a kid stuck a foot out so she'd trip. For her, these were mean little third-graders. It wasn't always the kids at school. There was the time my neighbor and once babysitter who was somewhere between the age of 17 and 18 held me down, pulled her pants down, and farted repeatedly in my hair. My hair literally smelled like shit afterward, not to mention she almost broke my neck. She wasn't by any means a small or skinny person and I was a scrawny kid.

My aggression grew out of the feeling that I had to find ways to protect my sister and myself, or perhaps it was the separation from my father and the sense of displacement. The feeling of being lost and having zero control. All of those pent-up emotions led me to always be on the defense, always ready to fight. I remember fighting my neighbor and dragging her by her long thick pigtails through a mud-covered courtyard. Or going up the side of Tyrone's head (another neighbor kid) with a rock for bothering my sister. I legit bashed him in the left side of his head, leaving blood and dirt on him. My sister, by the way, had once pushed this same kid off a two-story balcony. Needless to say, she didn't need me to defend her, but I always tried to fiercely protect her. Sadly during this time, I had become so violent and impulsive that even my sister at times could not escape my wrath. You could even say I bullied her from time to time too.

I've since apologized to my sister for allowing my internal pain to inflict external pain upon her. She laughed it off and told me she knows I was angry and that it was okay. I accept that she accepts me as I am and as I was, but what still tugs at my heart just a little, is that I feel I should've been a better big sister to her. Back then, it felt like we were all we had and although I forgive myself, I wish I'd had the capacity to realize this sooner. Fear can turn you into many things. Fear made me violent.

Now here's my karma, lol. My sister is five inches taller than me and she's stacked! She is strong, solid, and has a longer arm span than I do. I'm 5'3" and 120 pounds. I'm a petite little woman and in our teens and 20s, Jas has gotten me back a time or two. We haven't argued or gotten into it since our early 20s, but I'd bet on Jas winning in a boxing match!

Dear Jasmine,

We've talked through our childhood before, and you've already expressed forgiveness and laughed off my "mean big sister" treatment of you. You even explained that you understood it was a hard time for us and didn't hold my behavior against me. I love the forgiving person you are and still, I feel I could've been a better sister to you in the past. I want you and every reader to know how truly sorry I am for any time I've hurt you mentally, physically, emotionally, or otherwise. I love you with all of my heart. You're such an amazing young woman and mother. I'm grateful to have the opportunity to share my life with you every day. Thank you for forgiving me, believing in me, and always being by my side.

(Jasmine, *on the left*, and I preparing for Hartford, Connecticut, Caribbean Carnival 2014)

I did not win every fight. I was certainly always ready to fight, but I'm no MMA fighter and got my ass handed to me a few times. The award for most memorable childhood beatdown goes to a girl named Joy. The reason for the fight remains unclear, but the ass-whopping remains vivid. Just like a typical schoolyard fight scenario, it all started at lunch. I don't know what was said, but Joy and I were scheduled to hash out our differences at recess. I threw the first punch with confidence and watched it land across her face as we were surrounded by our peers yelling and egging us on, away from the watchful eyes of monitors and teachers. I thought I had won, the punch and the landing seemed victorious. Before I knew it, I was eating wood chips as Joy knocked me to the ground and made me realize that perhaps I'm not the only one who knows how to use their fists to make a statement.

Not long after the fight, Joy and I became friends. Fortunately we were able to forgive each other, and I avoided getting beat up in front of my fifth-grade class again. I did manage to make a couple of friends here and there, even with all the moving around from Connecticut to Alabama. Later that year, I met Nicole and her family.

Nicole and I would do lots of things together, which is probably why I remember her so much. Nicole's parents would take us to the mall or she and I would go for walks around her suburban neighborhood. Once we even went to the Town Fair! My love for carnivals and fairs began that day. As always, there was so much to see and do at the fair! Rides, games, and delicious snacks. We all know there's nothing better than candied apples, popcorn, cotton candy and for Nicole, boys. She was always talking to and getting the attention from boys. I liked boys too but they weren't interested in me as much as they were in Nicole.

Nicole did not have the body of most kids our age. She wasn't flat-chested or skinny like I was. To me, Nicole looked like she could be at least 17, and that's exactly the type of guys who would approach her when we were out together. The boys were always older, always asking questions or engaging in conversations that I didn't quite understand. I didn't care what Nicole was doing or talking about with those boys. I was always just happy to have a friend.

At our first sleepover, I definitely thought her parents were a little rich. Who else do you know had a TV projector AND a Blu-Ray disc player in 1998, just in their den?! To me, goddamn rich people, that's who. I had just heard about DVDs and DVD players, and *they* had the exclusive Blu-Ray disc player in their house! I didn't even tell you about the family transport. Nicole's father drove this tricked-out family van, fully equipped on the inside. I'm talking TV screens, climate control, LED lighting along the floor, leather seats, the works! It was amazing. Their home was no different. Beautiful and spotless with all the bells and whistles! By no means was their home a mansion or anything like that, but they had a nice-ass suburban, middle-class home. For what my living experiences had been like in Alabama up until that moment, I was in awe.

Nicole even had a bathroom IN her room! Her very own personal bathroom AND walk-in closet. Shit, she had her own room. She had more than I ever saw or had at that time in my life. My sister and I had a roof over our heads and food in our bellies, but we didn't exactly have proper beds at the time. Jasmine slept on a cot, and I slept on a pallet on the floor next to her. Nicole's plush, pillowy, queen-sized bed looked like a dream! I felt like the princess and the pea as I climbed up into her bed searching for the perfect spot to get comfortable.

It didn't take long for us to figure out what we wanted to watch. Nicole already had something in mind and she was insistent. *Starship Troopers!* A 1997 science fiction/action film where the earth is at war with a race of giant alien insects. Fun fact: Science fiction/action is probably my favorite genre. *The Fifth Element* is one of my top-five favorite movies. I wasn't a huge fan of *Starship Troopers*. It was insanely gory and violent, and there was nudity and implied sex, which was unfamiliar terrain to me up until that movie and that night.

As we lay in bed side by side flinching as we watched images of shattered corpses, she took my hands and guided them along her body, up to her breasts. She motioned for me to rub them as I lay otherwise completely still and confused as to what we were doing. *"Is this normal sleepover behavior?"* I wondered. This was my first real sleepover. *"Do all friends do this at sleepovers?"* I allowed her to use my hands to touch her breasts and vagina. I didn't quite understand what was going on or exactly what we were doing, but I did it. Following that night, I didn't see much more of Nicole that summer.

After that night, it seemed unwanted and confusing sexual encounters coupled with curiosity became the norm for me. My curiosity or need to talk to an adult was probably never greater at any time in my adolescent life than the summer between fifth and sixth grade. Curiosity and lack of knowledge led to exploration which in some cases led to situations that I, as a fifth-grader, had no business being in.

With my son now in sixth grade, I want to take a moment to encourage parents to talk to their children about sex and also, yes, in my opinion, be a little cautious of sleepovers. This is not just because of sexual exploration. There are a ton of reasons I could list, but that might be another book.

After my experience with Nicole, I found myself bewildered but also a bit curious. What did that interaction mean? Was it normal? I had a lot of unanswered questions. How does a kid explore something they want to know more about without asking their parents? They either ask their friends, a trusted adult, or search the internet.

When I was in fifth grade, we didn't own a computer or have regular access to the internet. I didn't have an adult I could talk to about sexual things. But we did have cable. I took to cable television and found out about Cinemax and HBO After Dark with show ratings including nudity and strong sexual content, looking for answers. I even stumbled upon pornography on Pay-per-view and was caught on more than one occasion watching it. Truthfully, I just wanted to understand what all of this touching and feeling was supposed to be.

REALITY CHECK

When it comes to my own son, I don't have all the answers but I will do my best to practice openness with him and have honest conversations about life, love and sex. Things like consent, safety, and being ready to take a big step like engaging in sex.

As parents we can't control everything that our children will see, do, or have access to, but we can prepare them. If I had been more prepared, there's a chance I would have made different decisions for myself along the way. While I may not have made the best decisions in the past, I write these words as a reminder of the decisions I will continue to make now and in the future for myself and my family.

If you're a parent, sibling, aunt, uncle, or cousin to a younger person, stop and think about what you can teach this young person to help prepare them for the world. Ask the question, *"Is there anything you'd like to talk about?"* That simple question can make a world of difference. Most of all, teach your children to speak up for themselves. Today I help my son build his confidence by encouraging him to express himself and share how he feels so that if he is ever in a situation where he feels uncomfortable, he has the courage and the tools to speak up and voice his discomfort or concern. I practice listening to him and validating his concerns.

Can you think of someone in your life who could use your support? Perhaps a young person who could use an ear to listen to them or guidance from a more experienced person? Our children are the future. If we don't use our knowledge of the world and lived experience(s) to help guide them, we're missing a crucial step. We're missing the opportunity to positively impact their upbringing and help them develop into who they will become. We've all had experiences that when shared may help someone else. Practice that conversation by using the space below to jot down what you would like to talk to a young person about. Collect your thoughts and then share them.

Speak

_____

_____

_____

_____

_____

_____

_____

_____

_____

_____

_____

_____

CHAPTER III:
BACK & FORTH

IN SIXTH GRADE we moved again, this time into a bunga-
low-style home in downtown Birmingham, Alabama,
with our mom's boyfriend whom we had grown to like
and love very much. David was cute and fun to be around.
Every time David would visit mom when we lived at our
old apartment complex, all the girls in the neighborhood
wanted to come over just to see him. He was that type of
handsome. He had chocolate-skin and a smile that would
light up any room. To top it off, he was kind and he always
played games with my sister and me. He often felt like
more of a big brother than a stepdad. Regardless, we loved
having him around, and we were happy to move from
the apartments and into the new place with both mom
and David.

The new neighborhood was a bit janky and a little dingy
but we had a house, even if it was adjacent to a home with
boards on the doors and windows. I didn't like the fact that
there were bars on our windows, but Jasmine and I had our

own rooms. We even had a room dedicated to playing our PlayStation, complete with two reclining chairs and a big-screen TV. We had a lot of space, and it was nice to have a home.

One afternoon, David brought home an adorable chocolate brown pitbull puppy. She was so sweet, playful, and full of energy. We named her "Dirty" because of her brown coat and kept her in the backyard shed. For once in a really long time, it almost felt like I was part of a normal family.

I attended sixth grade in two places that year. The first few months I attended Wilkerson Middle school. I had to walk quite a distance back and forth to school, around 20 minutes each way in the scorching Alabama sun. It was already HOT outside by 7 a.m. I absolutely hated that walk, and I wasn't a fan of the school. I felt displaced, anxious, and on edge.

Up until middle school, my sister and I had always attended school together. Maybe it was the shock of being separated or just fear, but I felt I didn't fit in and I was always crippled with that fear. I was scared of being bullied, scared of making friends, and scared of not making it home on those long school walks. Thank God David would pick me up from school sometimes. We'd go grab fast food, usually KFC or Church's Chicken, and head to his mom's house. I loved his Mom. She was welcoming and sweet. She used to let my sister and me help her make her famously delicious cakes. I still smile when I think about those moments.

In September of 1999, my mom's youngest sister Aunt Nita married our Uncle George. They had been together for as long as I can remember, since 1992 as a matter of fact. He was our uncle and a member of the family long before they were officially married. Thank God for their wedding because we got to go back home to Connecticut.

After nearly two years, we were reunited with our father and immediate family. Mom's older sister Aunt Debra visited us once in Alabama with her daughter and our cousin Nesha. Yet nothing compared to going back to Connecticut and being surrounded by family, familiar faces, and the people you love.

Once we were back in Connecticut, we begged our mom to stay. After much pleading and convincing talks with her

Left to Right: Me, Nesha, and Jasmine, in Alabama in 1997

and dad, she agreed and we were enrolled in Silver Lane Elementary School. Mom returned to Alabama and we stayed in our home in East Hartford with dad. Although I was happy to return to what felt like normalcy, this time my mom was gone.

My dad took on parenting us as best as he could. He started working the night shift before retiring later that year and enlisted our cousin Cynthia and our Aunt Charlene, who lived next door, to help care for us. Fun fact: In Connecticut, we lived on a cute cul-de-sac of duplex homes. My aunt lived to the right of us. The future father of my son lived two houses to the left, but that's another story. My sister's best friend Katiria lived next door to my son's father, and my friend Taina lived across the street from her. Next door to Taina was our childhood friend Danielle and her family. It was a pretty close-knit neighborhood. For the most part, everyone's parents knew each other and all the kids hung out or played with each other.

Before starting at our new school, dad took us on a shopping spree at Burlington Coat Factory and Walmart. Our new school didn't require uniforms, and dad let us pick out all of our new clothes and school supplies. My new notebooks, folders, and pencils were covered with the faces of The Backstreet Boys (BSB). I'd like to hope all of my readers know who BSB is but in the event some don't, BSB is arguably one of the greatest pop boy bands of the

1990s to early 2000s. I was a fan then, and I remain a fan now. What I was not a fan of was yet another school transition. The pros: Familiar terrain, access to dad, and other family nearby. The cons: New school, new people, and readjusting. We spent two years without our dad and now our mom had returned to Alabama. *"How long would she be gone?"* I wondered.

Of course in the beginning of the school year, I had an interesting time trying to adjust. I was often made fun of by classmates because of my accent. In class we'd regularly take turns reading excerpts from our assignment out loud. I always loved to read but I didn't particularly enjoy reading out loud, especially with the accent I picked up in Alabama. I didn't sound anything like anyone else in class anymore and I was reminded every time it was my turn to read. I could barely get through a sentence before one asshole kid, Jonathan, would begin to mimic my every word as the class slowly erupted into roaring laughter. I 'd sit there feeling embarrassed, fighting back tears and wanting to punch him, simultaneously. The teacher could never kick him out of class quite quickly enough if you asked me.

If school wasn't annoying enough, my dad started dating. Why would he date when we had just gotten back home? I hadn't seen my dad for years and now I had to share our time with him with some woman. I did not take kindly to Tammy the way my sister did. Don't get me wrong, she wasn't mean or anything, I just wasn't feeling her. Tammy and Jasmine got along great. Two peas in a fricken pod. She and I did not connect, and I was deeply uninterested in connecting with her. I didn't like or trust her. She was more than 30 years younger than my dad. He was retired and always available. I thought it was complete bullshit and I was still team "mom," not that I ever expected my mother and father to get back together but because I didn't want another woman trying to replace my mother. She wasn't dead, she was just in another state. Tammy was not much older than me and I didn't feel the *need* to respect her.

I thought that coming back to Connecticut and returning to the familiar would be easy but a lot of it wasn't. At times I found myself longing for and missing my low-key nomadic mom, sometimes missing Alabama. There is something about the South that is truly mesmerizing and captivating. It could be the Southern hospitality or the unceasing sun. Although the South is known to be riddled with racism—especially the deep South places like Alabama, Louisiana, and Mississippi—still, there's something about being surrounded by people who look like you.

Everywhere I turned there was a beautiful sea of brown skin, at least in my neighborhood in Alabama. The state is nearly 30% Black versus Connecticut, which is about 9%, and where we lived in Alabama felt like 88% Black. It was like nothing I'd ever seen or experienced in all my life.

That stark demographic contrast captivated me and connected me to Alabama despite how difficult it truly was to be there. A piece of that place attached itself to my heart, *and* my mom was there.

It wasn't until I moved back to Connecticut that I began to receive negative cues or comments about the color of my skin. In Alabama dark-skinned, light-skinned, and brown-skinned people were everywhere, but here I stood out. I was undeniably the darkest person in my class and the darkest kid on my street. People seemed to constantly remind me that I was Black or dark-skinned, as if mirrors didn't exist and I didn't already know.

Some kids would even insinuate that my sister and I weren't related because I was so much darker than she was. Granted kids can be real jerks, but hurtful words didn't always come from just kids. Parents can be hurtful too. Whenever I'd get in trouble, my dad would always refer to me as Black-Ass or Dark-Ass. I remember thinking, *"Why do you always have to bring that up?"* I never understood why skin tone was always a topic and there was too much emphasis on the word "BLACK."

Internally I began to associate my blackness with "ugly" or "bad" because my skin never seemed to be associated with anything "positive" or "good." Dad never reminded my sister Jasmine of her skin color, so why was I always reminded? It made me feel partly like I wasn't seen, all that was visible was my darkness that I had no control over. Words can have control over your mind. Those words from the man I revered and longed to be around really impacted me and primed me to believe there was nothing good about how I looked. I felt alone, confused, misunderstood, and above all, invisible.

We lived in a quaint cul-de-sac. In our neighborhood pretty much everyone knew each other. Even Tammy's family lived next door to Taina's. Everyone really did know everyone to the point that if someone new moved in or if there was someone new on the street, it didn't go unnoticed.

I remember it was a warm day, a little muggy even, so it must've been early summer when this guy moved into the home across the street from Taina's house. I still remember what he wore that day: White tee, baggy dark blue jeans, and sneakers. Taina, Shivonne, and I were sitting on the porch, watching them move in while playing M.A.S.H. to predict our futures, when he called us over.

MASH stands for Mansion Apartment Shack House. To find out which one of those dwellings you're going to live in someday, and other things like what kind of car you'll drive and who you'll marry, and how many kids you may have, you have to play MASH! MASH can be played with just a pen, paper, and a friend. Once you've filled in your options, you can choose a number between 1-10. For example, if I choose 8, I will go across

M.A.S.H.

BOYS	JOBS	PLACE
1.	1.	1.
2.	2.	2.
3.	3.	3.
4.	4.	4.

FRIENDS		PETS
1.		1.
2.		2.
3.		3.
4.		4.

KIDS	VEHICLE	COLOR
1.	1.	1.
2.	2.	2.
3.	3.	3.
4.	4.	4.

the entire paper counting one through 8 and crossing out an option every time I reach 8 until I have only one option left for each section, sealing my final fate!

I remember instantly thinking, "*He's definitely not talking to me. He must be talking to Taina or our other friend.*" I had accepted the fact that I was not pretty. I was dark-skinned, skinny, and flat-chested. My friends were beautiful. Taina was Puerto Rican with shoulder-length brown hair, and she had this amazing athletic gymnast figure. She'd been a gymnast since the age of 4. She was graceful, strong, and bilingual. How could I compare to that? Our other friend Shivonne was tall with almond-brown skin, long thick black hair that fell around her shoulders, bolstered by an incredibly beautiful smile with perfectly straight white teeth. Unlike Taina and me, she wore a real bra so he MUST be talking to the one of us with the bra, I thought.

He kept waving at us to come over but we decided that even if he was calling her, she wouldn't go over to him alone, so we all went. He asked us how old we were and I'm pretty sure we all lied a tiny bit, except maybe Taina.

I don't remember exactly what Taina said, but I know she had the most sense out of all of us. She didn't want to go over or talk to him at all! As predicted, he asked for Shivonnes' number. Of course, she didn't give it to him. I always admired her strength. Her ability to say no without wavering. She was very good at standing her ground. I wasn't strong like her and I admired that about her, envied it even. Everything I felt, I generally just kept it inside. Even if I wanted to say *"No,"* I often found it difficult. The art of displeasing someone and being okay with it was not a skill that I had acquired yet.

"I'll see y'all around," he told us after Shivonne turned down his advances.

We laughed back to Taina's porch and talked about how cute he *wasn't* and how old we thought he might *actually* be in comparison to the age he gave us. Although we unanimously decided he was gross and smelled weird (it was weed, an unfamiliar scent at that age), there was a part of me that was somewhat jealous. At home, I felt unwanted, out of place, and at times unnoticed. My dad was dating, my mom was gone. Jasmine was friends with Tammy. Where did I fit into that? I didn't.

A few days later, Taina and I were sitting outside on her front porch again. It was a cloudier day but still warm. I looked out across the street and there he was, eyeing Taina and me as we chatted playfully with each other. He motioned for us to come talk to him again, but Taina was not having it and made it clear to me that she wasn't going.

"I'll just go over and talk to him to see what he wants," I told her.

With wide eyes, she begged me not to cross the street, practically pleading with me as if she knew something would happen. I didn't listen. I smiled at her as I stood up with her hand in mine.

"Everything will be okay," I insisted as I dropped her hand and proudly walked across the street.

I walked over and said *"Hi."* He told me I looked nice and asked me my age again. I guess he was pleased by my response, because he said he would give me $20 if I followed him and kissed him on the lips. I nodded in agreement and he motioned for me to follow him, and I did, as Taina stood across the street watching us.

I ran over to her and told her, *"I'll be right back, don't worry. I'm just going to go around the corner with him, right quick, I won't be far."*

I followed him up to the corner of our cul-de-sac and across the street. We slipped behind these extremely tall tree-like bushes that line the Department of Transportation (DOT) facility across the street from our cul-de-sac. The proximity of the DOT was a blessing in the winter months. Our street was always first up for snow removal!

We stepped behind those bushes and immediately all the bravado I had to walk across the street and follow this at least

19-year-old young man transformed into paralyzing fear. I didn't know what was about to happen, but I held onto the fact that Taina was still waiting for me as my guiding light.

We stood behind the bushes facing each other. I could barely look him in the eyes. I lowered my head and immediately held out my hand, expecting a crisp $20 bill to be placed in my palms.

"I'm going to get it from my cousin when we go back," he told me.

I lowered my hand and stood in complete silence. He then lifted my chin and kissed me on my lips as I stood motionless and practically breathless. He stepped back.

"Take this off," he said as he went for the spaghetti straps on my shirt.

He slowly pulled down the straps of my shirt to examine my childlike body because that's exactly what it was. I was as straight as a board. I hadn't even gotten my period yet. He touched my nipples with his fingertips and I immediately pulled my shirt up and told him *"I need to leave, Taina is waiting for me."* I could feel the tears beginning to well up in my eyes. He seemed to notice my discomfort so he tried to reason with me.

"I'll give you $50 if you stay for five more minutes." But of course, he'd have to get it from his cousin first. I again shook my head in agreement, as I watched him pull down his pants and show me his penis.

I had never seen a penis in real life. Sure I saw glimpses of the male member on TV, but not like this. I was horrified and grossed out. To this day, I get a nauseous feeling in the pit of my stomach whenever I tell this story. He put my hands on his penis and again I froze up. I can never forget the feeling of the warm skin in my small hands as he moved my hands along him. I fought not to vomit with every centimeter of that thing that I was introduced to. He then turned me around where I stood and pulled my pants down. I could feel the warmth of his body against me. His breathing changed. It slowed as his hands gripped my tiny biceps as he tried to force me into position to enter me. I squeezed my bottom so tight there was no way he was getting into anything but, my GOD was he trying to pry me apart.

"Stop squeezing," he told me.

"I'm not," I lied as I continued to clench my body with all my might, praying that he wouldn't try to turn me around or find another way to do whatever it was he wanted to do.

He must've fought with me and my body for about three minutes until finally, he gave up. I felt him back away from me seemingly disappointed as I stood with my back to him shivering with fear under the summer sun. He promised me he'd come back with my money. He told me to wait for 10 minutes and disappeared through the bushes. I don't know how long I stayed there but, after some time, I pulled myself together and emerged from the bushes. I ran straight to Taina's house. I didn't tell her anything at all. I just cried.

She begged me to tell her what happened, but I couldn't and wouldn't speak. I also didn't really understand what happened. I wasn't raped. I agreed to go with him. I wanted to go with him. I didn't understand what I was doing or getting myself into and over the course of my life, my relationship with boys and men and sex continued to be very confusing. Not every moment with men and sex is filled with remorse, confusion and FEAR, but a lot of it was.

At school the next day, Taina told our friend Shivonne that something happened to me but she didn't know what happened because I wouldn't talk. One or both of them must've told our teachers because in the middle of recess, I was called to the principal's office.

About 100 questions were thrown at me by the nurse, the principal, and police officers. They even called my dad. The pressure broke my silence as I began to describe to them what had happened to me, what he looked like, and where he lived. By the time I got home that day, there were police officers at his house. I watched from the living room window as he was placed in the back of the police cruiser. I wanted to shrink inside myself with everything I had caused that summer. After graduating from sixth grade, I returned to Alabama to live with my mom. Just me this time, no sister and no dad.

It has taken me many years and many sessions of therapy to stop blaming myself for the sixth- grade incident, as I warmly refer to it. It was hard to accept what happened to me as molestation because I blamed my 12-year-old self for seeking attention. I blamed myself for the results of what seeking attention got me. A grown man's penis in my hands at the age of 12.

One thing that helped me let go of the notion that it was my fault and I'm just this overly sexualized person was therapy. My therapist taught me more about our prefrontal cortex. Our prefrontal cortex is the part of the brain responsible for skills like planning, prioritizing, decision-making, and controlling impulses. The prefrontal cortex is one of the last regions of the brain to mature. Some scientists believe it takes up to age 30 for this area of the brain to become fully mature.

I was a child who did not have an understanding of the long-term implications of my actions. On the other hand, a young adult around the age of 19 certainly had a greater understanding of what he was doing to me. It took me over a decade to unlearn the negative story of my molestation that I taught myself.

I don't know if I ever thanked Taina for what she did for me. She truly tried to keep me out of harm's way. She offered me as much support as a child and friend could offer. She followed her instincts and confided in trusted adults. As a result of her actions, I was provided with closure from this and a sense of safety. I watched from my living room window as the police went to my attacker's house. I saw them leave with him in their car, and I learned that what happened was wrong. Yet I was still impacted by the wrong that occurred. I never talked about it until I met my therapist and started writing this book. I had always glossed over my molestation as if it just happened to me and that was it. I never took the time to think about how much that day impacted my life. That day, like many other days, changed me and rocked the core of my soul. I finally found the courage to face that day head-on and talk about it.

Dear Taina,

Thank you for being a true friend. You do not come by true friends often in life, and your loyalty has always been unmatched. Thank you for trying to protect me and for caring for me in ways that span beyond friendship. You were like family to me. You were always nice to me, and you always listened to me. You became a sister to me at a time when I felt I had no one and didn't fit in. I fit in with you. Thank you for being there and for loving me the way you did.

With love,
Brittainy

REALITY CHECK

I challenge you to reflect on a time when there was the opportunity to thank someone for helping you, but you never
quite got the chance. This is your moment to practice gratitude by showing appreciation and returning that kindness,
in your own words. I encourage you to take the time to
show gratitude to that individual.

Dear, _____

_____

_____

_____

_____

_____

_____

_____

CHAPTER IV:
STICKS & STONES

L IFE WAS A lot different when I returned to Alabama. Mom's boyfriend, David, was no longer in the picture. Mom, on the other hand, seemed to be doing just fine. She had moved on up and now we lived at Riverchase Apartments in Hoover, Alabama. Our new home was modern. We had a balcony, two bedrooms, and two bathrooms. Mom had a walk-in closet and an ensuite bathroom. The apartment complex was equipped with all the bells and whistles: multiple pools, tennis and basketball courts. There was a fitness room, where I spent a lot of my time attempting to exercise and watching TV. We didn't have cable in our apartment, so I often found myself in the fitness center watching MTV.

We lived in a quiet picturesque suburban neighborhood surrounded by other modern apartment homes. Hoover is the largest suburban city in Alabama and known as the "Heart of Dixie.'" It is popular for the Riverchase Galleria Mall, which covers an area of over 2 million square feet and has more than 140 stores. The Galleria is the largest shopping mall I've ever seen.

Hoover is also a football town. Hoover high's football players were once featured on an MTV special titled *Two-A-Days*, a reality show that chronicled the lives of teens and focused on the school's highly-rated Hoover Buccaneers football team. Hoover had great public schools which, according to my mom, was the reason she moved there. She wanted me to have the opportunity to attend a good school in a good town, but it didn't quite turn out that way.

Mom worked two jobs, which explained why she was able to afford our ritzy apartment in Hoover. She worked in an office during the day and part-time in the food industry some nights. She always brought home delicious food and sweet tea for me. I enjoyed our new dwellings and it was wonderful to have such a nice place to live in, but it would've been nicer if my mom was home with me more often. She was never able to take me to the bus stop in the mornings, and she was almost never there when I returned from school in the afternoon. When the bullying began, I had no one in my immediate surroundings to turn to. My mom was often working, my sister was hundreds of miles away and still in elementary school. *"What help could they be to me?"* I thought.

That first day of school was nothing short of terrifying. Due to some weird zoning laws, the kids in my neighborhood were not allowed to attend Berry Middle School or Hoover High School, which were literally five minutes away. Instead we were bussed out about 30 or 40 minutes to McAdory School in McCalla, Alabama. Now if you ask me, there was some racism/classism shit going on, but I was too young to understand or ask questions. All I knew was my mom was pissed with my having to attend that school, especially when she moved to that area *specifically* so I could attend better schools. Not only was I bussed outside of town, but the middle school and the high school were also connected and it included grades 6-12. This was a complete shocker to me. At home in Connecticut, elementary school ended in grade 6. Middle school consisted of grades 7 and 8, and then there was high school. What the hell was this?

I still remember the first bus ride to my new school. Long, mildly lonely, and a little exciting.

I plopped down in my seat and gazed out of the window as the suburban city of Hoover transformed into wooded country. Houses began to drift further and further apart as trees took back their natural place in nature, enveloping the land as we made our way. There was a friendly white girl on the bus who greeted me each morning, her blonde crown hovered over the seat in front of me. I'd sometimes stare at her reflection in my seat window to pass the time. Did I mention the bus ride was at least 30 to 40 minutes? That's only counting the stops I remember. Not to mention,

I was the second stop on the route so second to last to get home.

"*Hi*" she'd chime each time I got on the bus. "*Hi,*" I'd respond, nervously. Of course, at the sound of my Northern accent, her eyes widened and the questions began to flow from her lips like the Mississippi River. Where are you from? How old are you? What grade are you in? Where is your family from? Why do you live here? Do you like it here? Sometimes, she'd ask me to pronounce random words simply because she liked how each syllable rolled off my tongue sprinkled with my "up North accent." The blonde girl on the bus was always nice to me. I don't remember her name, but I never forgot her kindness.

I often found that my accent was quite the spectacle at my new school. I was frequently asked by my peers to repeat words. "Proper" is what I was often referred to as because of my accent, and I didn't mind. I learned very early in life how to switch my accent on and off to adapt to my surroundings in an attempt to fit in or protect myself from those who thought the way I sounded deserved ridicule rather than curiosity.

Later in life, I learned that this behavior of going back and forth with my accent is called "code-switching." Code-switching is the act of modifying your speech, behavior, or appearance to adapt to different social or cultural norms. By Middle School I had mastered this strategy.

McAdory School was quite big, especially in comparison to Silver Lane Elementary School back home in Connecticut. Not only was the school massive, but coming in as a new seventh-grader from another state and from elementary school was shocking and scary.

Once we arrived at school, all the students poured out of the buses and into the gymnasium. I had never seen a gymnasium of this magnitude, filled to the brim with pre-teens and teenagers. It was more like entering an arena than a school gym. I nervously tightened my grip on the straps of my book bag, feeling completely overwhelmed and out of place. Fear was oozing from my pores and it must have been evident. The mean girls sniffed me out right away and within the first week of school, the bullying began.

First it was the taunting. Then there was the exclusion followed by heckling. Finally the threats. To this day, I still don't understand why or how I became the target of this group of individuals, but I was. I often wondered, *"What did I do or say to make them treat me differently?"* Was it my clothes or my accent? Was it because I was so quiet?

I found that throughout my various school experiences there was a recurring theme around my dialect, speech, or accent that often led to bullying. It's sad and disheartening to know something as small as an accent can negatively impact someone's life to the extent it did mine. I can't imagine what someone with an accent from another country might endure at the hands of children and unhealed adults.

Later in ninth grade when I attended an inner-city high school, my suburban accent caused a lot of ridicule. I wasn't Black enough for the Black kids or I sounded too Boujee. I was often referred to as an "oreo" or accused of acting and sounding white. Somehow the way I spoke was equated to people assuming that I thought I was better than my own. Unbeknownst to them, I had my own struggles. By no means was my life easy because I sounded a certain way.

One morning as I walked into the zoo of a gymnasium, I noticed a group of Black girls sitting on the bleachers to the right of me. I watched them briefly, longing to be part of any friendship circle and missing the friends I'd left behind in Connecticut. I wasn't able to avert my gaze quickly enough before one of them noticed and gave me an unwelcoming stare. I tried to nonchalantly look away. Her head snapped back to her group of friends, then I heard it, "Ugly Bitch" and an uproar of laughter as they all looked my way. I smiled politely and moved to another area further away from their line of sight, silently hoping that comment wasn't directed at me. I attempted to rationalize in my head who else they might have been talking to. Was I staring so long that perhaps I began daydreaming and imagined they were talking to me? After all, why would anyone call me a bitch if I hadn't done anything to them or I didn't know them? So maybe they weren't talking to me, right?

The bell rang and I hung back to make sure the group of girls left before heading to class. As far as I can recall, I hated most of my classes except one: music. It was in music class that I actually talked to someone besides the blonde girl on the bus. Her name was Tasha. We sat next to each other every day, and she always greeted me with a smile and conversation. Tasha may have been the closest thing I had to a friend that year. Not only were we in music together, I was blessed enough to have her in my science class too. Thank God for that because I felt like I had no one. We sat with each other in both classes, but the blessings stopped there. We didn't share a lunch period or any other classes, and I wished we had.

After the "Ugly Bitch" incident, each morning seemed to get increasingly worse. It started to feel as if the mean girls were waiting for me to enter the gym every day. One day as I walked into the gymnasium, I looked to the bleachers on my left and they all stood there staring at me menacingly, before turning to each other to say nasty things about me. Some days they shared their comments among themselves, leaving the element of wonder. Other days their comments bore a sense of pride as they hurled hurtful words at me loudly as I attempted to scurry by. Each morning, I jetted past them fearfully pretending to not hear a word. Pretending to not see them laugh at me or point at me, call me ugly, talk about my clothes, or where I was from. According to them, I was the skinny bitch from Connecticut who thought I was better than everyone else.

Lunch was arguably the lowest part of each day, except of course for the food. My GOD, the food was delicious. I had never had lunch like that. Every day at noon was Thanksgiving.

Even on my worst day, I knew the probability of an amazing meal was at least 90% likely. I grabbed the navy blue lunch tray and nervously got in line, silently watching the more experienced students around me assemble their lunches. I slid my tray along the metal counter as I was greeted by the sweet earthy smell of collard greens and sweet potatoes, accompanied by the protein options of pork chops or chicken *and* a side of cornbread. If you're not a lover of cornbread, there were different cakes and pies available to choose from. If that wasn't enough, there was an ice cream freezer with endless options and even a soda dispenser. This was by far the best lunch of my life I thought, as I paid for my meal excitedly.

Reality set in as I realized I'd have to find somewhere to sit and didn't have anyone to sit with. My eyes darted across the cafeteria frantically as I noticed empty spots at tables and attempted to find somewhere to blend in without seeming too alone or too eager. I headed over to a table of a group of girls who looked like me. It was a long bench table, not full, and I thought, maybe if I sat quietly at the end, I'll be okay. I put on a brave face, attempting to confidently walk toward the empty seat. The girls at the table seemed to notice me getting closer. Their glares met my determined eyes. I just needed to get to a seat, I thought to myself. I quickly scurried past them and made my way to the empty end of the table.

Many of my lunch periods weren't as easy as that one. As the weeks went by, something as simple as finding a seat for lunch became increasingly difficult. Naturally I gravitated to kids who looked like me, girls and boys with chocolate skin and kinky hair or braids.

It felt like I just kept making the wrong choices, approaching the wrong tables. I could no longer slide quietly into an empty bench at a lunch table without being told *"Someone is sitting there,"* or *"You can't sit there,"* but no one else was ever sitting there. These kids just wanted to make it clear to me that I had no place with them. I had food thrown at me while eating. I was even the victim on multiple occasions of the good old "stick your foot out and trip her" routine. It was embarrassing enough to be tripped by other students while carrying your lunch tray. Can you imagine if I ever fell? The embarrassment would've been devastating for me and likely invigorating for them.

Day after day, week after week there were persistent and aggressive threats, name-calling, and teasing. In the mornings, I would overhear these girls–and some boys whose names I can't recall–plotting to hurt me, jump me, or beat me up. My sheer existence seemed to be problematic for them, and I was clueless as to why.

Things took an abrupt turn for the worse when I noticed one of the boys and co-conspirators of my group of bullies was in my literature class. I didn't ever really notice him before because we had assigned seats earlier in the year. Once our teacher finally remembered all our names, we were able to sit freely.

In the classroom setting, I seldom had any issues. I even remember sitting by two white students who always wanted me to read things to them in literature class. There would be a random word or phrase that would come up in our reading and one of them would always turn to me and say, *"Hey Brittainy, can you pronounce that in your Connecticut accent?"*

I'd laugh and proceed with reciting the word or phrase. Even my teacher complimented me on my pronunciation, reading, and communication skills. Each day came with its own anxieties, yet I still found reasons to smile and in class, where I felt safe, I was always friendly to those who were friendly to me.

One day "Bully Boy" took the seat next to me in class. I was nervous as I watched him settling into his seat. I listened intently to the teacher, eyes forward, locked in on my lesson, avoiding the energy in the seat beside me. One day, after the teacher provided our classroom assignment,the class, myself included, began working diligently on our essays. The room fell silent with concentration. As I was writing, I felt a tap on my shoulder. I turned to my right to face him and surprisingly, all he did was ask for a pencil. *"Great,"* I thought to myself, relieved. This interaction seemed harmless. *"Maybe he's just a victim of groupthink,"* I thought *"and he's a better person outside of his group of mean friends."* Nope.

Our desks were configured in such a way that he was only about an arms length from me. I soon learned, an arm's length was far too close. He tapped me again and passed me a note. I opened the folded piece of paper to find the question, *"Are you a Ho?"* I can't say I knew what the word "Ho" meant at the time but I knew it wasn't necessarily a good thing and I knew I wasn't that. I ignored his message. I crumpled it up and continued to work on my assignment. He continued to pester me, and I continued to ignore him. I looked around for the teacher, who didn't seem to be paying attention to his behavior. No one seemed to be paying attention. He was poking me, whispering, and nobody seemed to bat an eye or move an inch. He then put his hands under the desk and started to grab and tug at my skirt.

I quietly tried to fight him off, slapping his hands but my actions only seemed to excite him. He was trying with all his might to get beyond my skirt and in between my legs. He pulled at my skirt and scratched my inner thighs as he tried to maneuver his dirty fingers closer to my underwear. It was as if the world around us stopped. Here we were in the classroom, middle of the fucking day and no one did anything.

I understand it is possible that people didn't see him, but it's also possible that they did and no one stopped him. I can still feel his fingertips digging and grabbing at me as I tried to get him to stop. I clasped my legs together tightly, but that didn't work. It only seemed to encourage him to work harder. I punched his hands, scratched his forearms, I even stabbed him with my pencil, but that didn't work. I whispered and pleaded with him to stop, but he simply would not.

He didn't stop until I bit him. I frantically snatched his hand, brought it to my mouth, and bit down hard until I could taste his blood. He laughed at me menacingly and snatched his hand from the grips of my teeth. Only then did I hear the teacher ask the class to quiet down.

When the bell rang, I rushed out of the classroom and straight to the bathroom to cry. What was I supposed to do in a school where I was being harassed daily? It had now escalated to sexual harassment, and I had the daily threat looming over me of a group of seven to eight girls and a few boys who seemed determined to make my life a living hell. It wasn't just the gymnasium or the lunch room. The fear and bullying had found its way into the only safe space I had–the classroom. I was no longer safe. How could the teachers not see what was happening? How could no one else say anything or think it was wrong? How did this happen to me in class? Did they think we were playing? What just happened to me at school?

"Bully Boy" told his friends and my arch enemies about the incident in class. The biting and the blood. I'm sure he'd left out the part about how exactly he got that bite. I'm sure he left out that I resisted and tried to fight back quietly as his hands forcibly tried to pry my legs apart as no one seemed to notice. If any did notice, they didn't care. I watched him in the gymnasium the next morning as he held up his arm to show the marks from my teeth that tore into his flesh a day before.

He seemed almost proud as he showed his friends what I had done, wearing the marks like medals as if this was the end game. They had somehow managed to steal a win from me. The fear they created had finally enveloped me whole. To make things worse, the rumor that was born from the agonizing experience was that I had somehow let him stick his finger in me, in class. That couldn't have been further from the truth. I was violated in front of a completely oblivious audience. There was no one to come to my aid. No one corroborated my story. There was just me suffering in silence, trudging through my pain, weighed down by what felt like torture at the hands of my peers. Each day at school became another day of trying to survive. I was able to move my seat in class, but I wasn't able to avoid my enemies at every moment of the day.

When I think of my middle school experiences in Alabama, I think of *The Karate Kid* reboot with Jackie Chan and Jaden Smith. Trey (Jaden Smith) is uprooted from the United States to China due to his mother's job transfer. In addition to the obvious language barrier, as he starts school, he's bullied pretty badly by a group of kids. It seemed like no matter what he did, his bullies always found him. They'd threaten him or beat him up. Treys' fights weren't regular schoolyard fights. His bullies were trained in the martial art of Kung Fu. Trey didn't know Kung Fu! How the hell does anyone defend themselves from a group of trained martial artists? Trey was ready to give up and declared he hated his life, hated China until he met Mr. Han, played by Jackie Chan. Mr. Han was the maintenance man in Trey's apartment building and a retired Kung Fu master. Mr. Han took Trey under his wing. He trained him, taught him discipline, and helped build his confidence. He also showed him love and compassion, and introduced him to the beauty of China and its culture. In the end, Trey was able to face his bullies in a Kung Fu Competition and *he won*. If only I'd had a Mr. Han to help me conquer my fears or face my bullies. Instead, I had to take matters into my own hands.

I sat down in class next to Tasha. This time, I was prepared for anything to happen. I had a purse with me and inside I carried notebooks, pens, pencils, and lunch money. Carefully wrapped in a small hand towel underneath the other items was a butcher knife. My weapon of choice to protect myself in the event anything were to happen to me that day. The daily likelihood of getting jumped was nothing new, but recently the threats seemed to become increasingly more dangerous and real. The dam could break at any moment and I knew I couldn't take them all, so I decided I'd bring a knife to help me fend them off. I never once thought about killing anyone. My plan was simply to scare them. I figured they wouldn't come near me if I pulled out this knife!

I opened my bag to show Tasha my knife. *"It's so they won't bother me anymore,"* I told her. *"You shouldn't have that,"* she told me coldly.

I noticed she was worried or maybe even scared. *"I won't* actually *stab anyone Tasha,"* I reminded her, *"but, I'll pull it out if they try to jump me. I have to and it's not for anyone else but them. Please don't tell,"* I begged her.

She silently nodded. I took a deep sigh of relief, closed my bag, and placed it under my desk. Before I could open my textbook in my next class, I was called to the principal's office. I didn't return to any classes that day. I ate my lunch in the principal's office, which I actually quite enjoyed. Between us, it may have been the best lunch day ever. For one, the security guard brought my lunch to me and although he only brought me milk for a drink, at least I didn't have to enter that cafeteria and look for a seat like a lost sheep.

I sat alone in the comfort of the office and attempted to explain why I had brought the knife, that I had no intention of seriously hurting anyone but that I was being bullied for months and I was afraid of what they might do to me. I even told him and other staff about the biting incident in class. All the students in my bullying ring and my only friend Tasha were interviewed. I don't remember if they were punished, but none of that truly mattered. At the end of the day, I was the one who decided to bring a weapon to school with the potential intent of harming another student.

According to Alabama knife laws, I could have been in major trouble. There are three types of illegal knives in Alabama. Illegal meaning, you cannot use, buy, sell, lend, or carry. This applies to both the citizens and the visitors of Alabama. One of those knives just so happens to be a butcher knife. According to the superintendent of schools, if the knife had been just a few inches longer, I would have faced time in a juvenile facility. Luckily, due to my mild disposition and in accordance with the law, I was expelled. The funny thing is that during my expulsion process, what I remember most is the superintendent's utter disbelief that *I* was the threat the school had painted me to be in the report he received. At first sight of me, he chuckled, and said, *"You're the little lady that's causing all this trouble. You look like you wouldn't hurt a fly."*

Generally, I wouldn't. I don't even like bugs, but given I was sexually harassed in front of a classroom and bullied daily for months, that type of traumatic experience might trigger a drastic response. So back to Connecticut I went to finish out seventh grade and rebrand myself.

REALITY CHECK

Let's take a moment to reflect on the extent of the bullying in this chapter. Writing this portion of the book was very eye-opening for me. When our children are at school, we as parents have a level of expectation that teachers, administrators, security guards, etc., will keep our children safe to the best of their ability. Unfortunately, I almost never felt safe at that school. I know it's hard to keep an eye on all the students, especially if the student-teacher ratio is 25:1 or some other ridiculously high number. Still it's scary to know that none of the adults were aware of the intense bullying that was happening to me nearly every day. Sure I could have spoken up, but there's still a level of attention that should occur for each student in a school setting for the purpose of safety and learning development.

My own personal experience with bullying led me to think about how we can find ways to make sure our children aren't neglected in the classroom. "Bully Boy," unfortunately, was able to do what he did to me partly because his behavior was often ignored. He was frequently misbehaving. He was one of those kids who the teacher was always calling on or yelling at to sit down or pay attention, or even dismissing him from class.

Therefore when he began disturbing the class that day and sexually harassing me, people just kept their heads down. It's likely the other students could have been frozen by the "Bystander Effect" that occurs when the presence of others discourages someone from intervening in a situation like bullying or in this case, an assault. As people, we need to pay more attention to each other. Parents to their children. Teachers to their students, managers to their employees, and so on. Talk to each other and ask questions. It truly takes a village, and we all must work together to create a community for the betterment of our future and our children's futures.

I challenge you to think of a time when you could have stood up for someone. Maybe you have experienced the bystander effect and had a moment where you thought, *"I should say something,"* but you didn't. What was that scenario and what would you do differently today?

_____

_____

_____

_____

_____

Speak

CHAPTER V:
FRIENDS: HOW MANY OF US HAVE THEM?

M AKING FRIENDS WASN'T necessarily hard for me, but making the right friends wasn't exactly easy. In middle school, high school, and even into my early 20s, I often found myself lost in a sea of individuality simply trying to find my way and find myself.

In seventh grade, once I returned to Connecticut, I attended East Hartford Middle School and became friends with two girls, Megan and Jessica. I guess you can consider them EMO. According to the stereotypes, EMO people are depressed, generally have dark hair, and have a certain style of dressing or music they may listen to. On the outside, one might say, we didn't have a lot in common but, regardless of their looks or style of dress, they were my friends.

I soon learned that they were a bit more hardcore than I expected, and I often found myself in trouble or in peculiar situations when we spent time together. Megan taught me how to shoplift, and I wasn't very good at it. We'd steal small items like makeup and costume jewelry from just about anywhere. The mall, grocery store, or local pharmacies. It wasn't long before my klepto antics caught up to me. I was arrested at the mall in 7th grade for stealing and was placed in the back of a police car. Thankfully I wasn't cuffed, but it was very embarrassing to be publicly cornered in the mall by security and of course, I was the only one of us who got caught.

I'm not sure if you've ever been in the back of a police vehicle but word of advice, don't plop down! I almost broke my damn tailbone sitting in the back of that car. Hard-ass vinyl! Looking back, there were so many things I did outside of my character just to fit in. I tried smoking cigarettes and drinking alcohol. I'm relieved I never became accustomed to any of those behaviors–stealing, drinking, and smoking cigarettes. It's not me and never was.

Megan had an older brother who was in high school. When I visited her, he often had friends over and they would drink, Megan included. I still remember the first time she offered me a shot of Goldschlager. Goldschlager is a nasty (in my middle-school-age opinion) cinnamon schnapps with gold flakes at the bottom of the bottle. Megan excitedly shoved the bottle at me and encouraged me to drink. Intrigued by the gold floaties at the bottom, I took a sip and immediately promised myself I'd never do that again. The taste was disgusting. *"Liquid death,"* I thought as it slid down my throat, burning every inch of my esophagus until it found my stomach. I couldn't understand how she seemed to enjoy alcohol and drink more of it but, if I had to guess, she was probably used to the taste. One sip was enough for me.

It seemed Megan's parents were very relaxed about certain things, like allowing their son to have friends over late during the school week or even drinking with his friends. I'm unsure if their parents knew but, in my house, there's no way I could've drank alcohol at home without my parents knowing.

Megan and her brother seemed to have so much freedom. All of this was unfamiliar terrain to me, along with the fact that Megan and Jessica were also cutters.

Cutting is when a person deliberately hurts themselves by scratching or cutting their body with a sharp object. The reasons someone might do this are complicated. I'd silently watch as Jessica and Megan dug into their arms and wrists with blades or other sharp objects. Jessica was often angry or upset with her mother when she did this. I won't lie, I was petrified internally when either of them took to their wrists in my presence. I asked them questions like, *"Does it hurt? Why are you cutting?"* Once they realized I wasn't a cutter, they started to encourage me to cut myself. Jessica even offered to do it for me, which scared the living shit out of me.

Honestly, I can't say I didn't try to cut, but I could never bring myself to do it. Sure, I was angry or upset about plenty of things but I suppressed all my feelings and held them inside or instead of cutting myself I'd carve things into walls. Things like, "I hate myself" or "No one loves me." These things were far from the truth but in my 7th grade mind they were an accurate depiction of how I felt at the time about myself.

Looking back, my biggest regret is that I didn't have the knowledge or understanding of what cutting was to truly offer either of them the help they may have needed at that time. After all, we were just kids. When my parents started to realize the changes in my behavior, I wasn't allowed to hang out with either of them anymore, eventually our friendship slowly faded away.

Eighth grade was a totally different ball game. I met Joeline and Amanda. They were my very best friends. We had so much fun together. I don't remember our fights or how we grew apart, but I certainly remember passing notes to Joeline in English class and sleepovers at Amanda's house. We'd eat brownies, stay up late, watch movies, and sit in her parents' jetted bathtub in our swimsuits and have girl talk. The three of us were inseparable.

If it wasn't for Amanda, I don't think I would've ever seen the comedy musical and romance film *Grease* or sit on a rooftop at night or even understand how to use a tampon.

If it wasn't for Joeline's family, it would have been nearly a decade before I had authentic Puerto Rican food. Joeline was loud, funny, and kind. I could tell her anything and she'd always listen. She had the most beautiful big brown eyes and dark curly hair. Amanda was my white girl with flavor! Her family was big and diverse. She was brunette with vibrant eyes that seemed to change color every time she changed her shirt. Just thinking of them brings me joy. Joeline and Amanda gave me exactly what I needed at that time in my teenage life. Fun friends.

During eighth grade, I applied to both Howell Cheney Technical High School (Howell Cheney Tech) and A.I. Prince Technical High School (Prince Tech). I was accepted into both. It felt amazing to be accepted into two schools. I had rocked both of my in-person interviews and between my good grades and warm personality, both schools wanted me. I made the choice to attend Prince Tech rather than Howell Cheney Tech or East Hartford High School. My mother, Aunt Debra, and Uncle Bobby all graduated from Prince Tech. I wanted to continue on in their footsteps and make practical decisions about my future. Attending a technical school, where I could learn a trade and seemingly work right after high school appeared to be the right choice.

High school and Prince Tech were nothing like I had imagined they would be. For one, Prince Tech is a large school located in the capital city of Hartford, Connecticut.

There were at least three floors, multiple wings, and plenty of places to lose your way. I could feel my anxiety setting in due to unfamiliar terrain. Here I was again, new school, new people, feeling totally out of my element. Yet this time around, finding a friend almost happened right away.

In ninth grade, I met Samantha. She and I grew to become very close. We shared a few classes together and we both chose a technical career in masonry. Samantha was like a big sister and best friend combo. She always looked out for me and was often giving me life advice, thwarting my bad ideas, or warning me about some of the other girls I hung around. Throughout my life, I've continued to learn the hard way about what a true friend actually is. But in ninth grade and to this day, one of the best examples I have of a true friend is Samantha.

Samantha was and remains funny as hell, tough as nails, and extremely charismatic. In high school, nobody messed with her and everyone respected her. Most days, I couldn't wait to get to class just to be in her presence. As I write, I reflect on how thankful I am for who she is, and who she was to me back then. As tough as she is, by nature she's a caretaker and protects those she loves. To this day, her character has not faltered. I've always admired her strength and resilience but most of all, I admire her authenticity, individuality, and genuine nature. From my vantage point, Samantha has always known who she is and that is what drew me to her, along with her sense of humor. Her energy and presence exude strength, not to mention all of her attributes are accompanied by a big, beautiful, infectious smile.

Samantha tried to keep me from getting involved with the wrong people at school. She warned me to be leery of one girl in particular. We'll call her "Tina." She was also in masonry and a bit more popular with the guys. Tina was considered to be a bit faster than Samantha and I. "Fast," according to the urban dictionary, refers to a girl or guy who is quick to engage in sexual activity. It certainly appeared that way, but I was never the judgemental type and though I may have been warned about her, I liked hanging out with her. We always had fun, but it almost always somehow turned sexual in one way or another when we were together.

The first thing she ever did that seemed odd to me occurred one day after school. We decided to walk to her house as we sometimes did. We'd often stop at C-Town, a local supermarket, for fresh warm bread from the bakery. Funny, I don't remember the type of bread it was, but it was always warm and delicious. Tina lived in a three-family home with her little brother and parents.

When we got to her house, she asked me if I wanted to see something funny and as some sort of cruel joke, she showed her four-year-old brother pornography on Pay-per-view and laughed about it. The poor kid had gotten so used to seeing porn that when she'd change the channel, he'd begin to cry and throw a tantrum. I honestly didn't know what to make of that and I didn't find it funny.

Tina always seemed hell-bent on helping me have sex with someone or anyone. It was almost as if she derived pleasure from encouraging others to commit sexual acts. Peer pressure is one thing, but her behavior was something different. Like lots of teenagers often do, I lied about my sexual activity to fit in with her. It seemed cool but in ninth grade, I was still a virgin. I pretended to be cool and sexually active, and it backfired.

One afternoon we were hanging out with some guys, playing video games. These guys either already graduated high school or went to a different school. Either way, they weren't ninth graders. Tina ended up leaving the house before me. I ended up making out with one of the guys and received my first hickey on my neck, but I did not have sex. After that afternoon, she suddenly began accusing me of sleeping with the guy. It turns out that the guy I had kissed and received the hickey from was the one she liked.

At school, Tina and one of her friends started bullying me, taunting me, yelling at me in the halls, and spreading rumors. As harmless or childish as this all sounds, once the bullying began it triggered a fear in me that was too painful to try and push through, so I ran. I didn't know what to expect or what to do, so I asked my mom if I could transfer to East Hartford High School. Just like that, I left Prince Tech.

In tenth grade, I enrolled in East Hartford High School (EHHS) and the school hopping finally ceased. EHHS wasn't perfect but my experiences there were far better than what I had gone through at most of the other schools. I had friends and met my best friend to this day, Katelyn, in my first year there. I played sports, including being the only female on the wrestling team in my junior year. I also played flag football. I worked at the school store. I was a member of the National Society of Black Engineers (NSBE). I sat with my friends every day at lunch. I even dated a guy who was pretty popular. EHHS was good to me and provided me with a pretty normal high school experience. Sure, it wasn't completely drama-free, but there was never a point where I recall feeling like I didn't belong. In 2006, I graduated alongside 200-plus other students in my class.

Following high school, I took some time to attend community college. While attending Manchester Community College in Manchester, Connecticut, I grew closer to my neighborhood friend and future father of my son. Before becoming a mother and dating my son's father, I continued to find my way. I didn't stop moving. In fact, if I hadn't become a parent, I'm certain I would have adopted a more nomadic lifestyle. When I was 19, I moved to Kissimmee, Florida, with my mother and her husband for a while. I worked at Disney World as a housekeeper. I dated both men and women since the age of 18. Throughout my journey, I found that I was attracted to both sexes probably around age 15. After spending some time in Florida, I applied to the University of Hartford (UHart) and headed back to Connecticut.

Home is where the heart is and upon returning to Connecticut, the fullness of my heart and being surrounded by friends and family kept me there. I attended UHart for a few semesters, but I was unable to continue due to a lack of funds and a clear understanding of what was available to me financially. I could go on for pages about my experiences at the UHART and how in just a short period of time, my view of myself changed. I began to see myself as an individual rather than someone who just blended in. I thoroughly enjoyed academics and was beginning to find my voice through education. I immersed myself in liberal arts. I loved finding ways to expand my mind beyond the normative or "thinking outside the box" as I'd often hear my professors say.

I dove head first into my literature and Western civilization classes. I sat at the very front of my Western civilization class, my hand was always shooting up ready to answer questions. I was so inspired by my professor, Dr. Gutierrez, that I was certain I was destined to be a professor just like him, teaching my students in exciting and engaging ways. Or I'd be like my drama professor, unapologetically flamboyant, everchanging, exceptional, educated, and non-judgemental, finding the beauty in every person's individual essence and encouraging students to simply "Be." I excelled as my mind was filled with ideas, knowledge, and encouragement passed on by my professors. Being at UHart made me feel alive in ways I've never felt. My mind was a sponge and my urge to soak my sponge was fierce.

I miss that feeling, that eagerness to sit in an auditorium and take notes. I was so passionate about my education because it invigorated me in a way that I never experienced in all my years of school, with the exception of gaining technical skills at Prince Tech. I still struggled with math, but I was great at everything else. I was the first person in my family to attend college. I signed the papers and attended, but my time was cut short. I didn't have a true understanding of the financial part, and that was a detriment to continuing my education at the time.

Life went on. I lived with my father for some time, working, partying, and dating until I became pregnant with my son, London. Naively, I thought having a child with someone naturally brought you closer together. For London's father and me, it only seemed to violently push us apart. All the stress caused by fights, lies, and battles over custody drove me in my mid to late 20s to want to find a way to manage the stress and change my life, not

79

only for myself but for my son. I wanted to let go and give it all over to GOD–the hurt from being a single parent, the confusion I felt about my sexuality, and all the pain I experienced both past and present. I needed to find a way to not succumb to all the negative feelings. I needed some respite and I wanted to show up the best I could for my son. I had always been close to religion by way of my mother and her mother, my Grandma Lucy. Grandma was always at peace, in my eyes. She often displayed so much love, understanding, and kindness. In fact, the family members on my mother's side who were Jehovah's Witnesses always displayed such calm and peace. I wanted that peace.

In my late 20s, I decided to return (I attended as a child) to the Kingdom Hall (Church of Jehovah's Witnesses). It was one of the best decisions I could've made for myself at that time. For one, returning to the hall gave me discipline. I attended Bible study Tuesday evening, service on Sunday morning, and personal Bible study at least once a week. Attending the hall as much as I did kept me from partying. Becoming "Sister Spencer" gave me a sense of community and brought me closer to my grandmother and other members of my family who were Jehovah's Witnesses.

If you've never been to a Kingdom Hall, I'll try to paint what a regular Sunday service might look like. Upon entering the doors everyone, and I mean everyone who is physically able, will be sure to say *"Hello."* Everyone will greet you with a gleam in their eye, a smile across their face, hands and arms outstretched, ready to embrace you or shake your hand. You would think there isn't one bad soul in the building based on their warmth and greetings alone. As you make your way to your seat, the ushers will kindly gesture to you open spots where you may sit. Everyone kindly speaks to their neighbor as the room continues to fill with familiar faces. No matter the color of your skin or ethnic background of individuals, we all refer to each other as "brother and sister." We refer to each other this way because we are all Jehovah's creations. We sing together, pray together, and study the Bible in unison.

Every Sunday for almost two years, I went to service. I was attending Tuesday studies regularly, and I progressed in my Bible study from simple knowledge to focusing more on application and moving on to baptism. I separated myself from past friends and lifestyles. I didn't want anything to distract me from creating peace and protection for myself and my son. I felt I found that in Jehovah. I found my community. I found safety, and I found peace. Then in one night, my entire life changed at the hands of a "friend."

Incoming text: *"We should really hang out! I miss you. I haven't seen you in a long time. You just got up and stopped talking to me."*

I knew she was right. Since I practically converted to a Jehovah's Witness a year prior, I kind of threw away a lot of my friends. According to my studies, many of my previous friends were engaging in worldly activities and immoralities. Things that would distract me from my path of righteousness.

She and I used to hang out ALL THE TIME. She was my road dog, my partner in crime, my girl, my trusted friend. The kind of friend that if I got drunk, she'd clean me up and put me to bed and keep me safe. The kind of friend who would argue with me loudly about our beliefs and differences, but it didn't change the love we had for each other. She was *that* type of friend.

When I changed my surroundings and my lifestyle, my interests changed. I was more focused on reading the Bible and preparing for service each Sunday. I no longer had a desire to do the things I used to do. I didn't go to parties. I didn't drink. Even my style of dressing changed. I had become demure and more reserved. Therefore I no longer saw her value in my life because drinking and partying were things we often used to do together. Reading her text though, I realized how much I missed her and our friendship, so I replied.

Outgoing text: *"Aww boo, you're right, and I'm sorry. How about Happy Hour?"*

Truth be told, I was excited to go out! Since I became active in the Kingdom Hall and was steadily progressing with my Bible studies, I was focused. My head was in the Jesus and Jehovah zone. After a while, I just stopped going out. Studying the Bible made the nightlife seem less appealing, which led to avoiding the scene altogether. Plus service was every Sunday at 9 a.m. and I had no desire to attend service tired or barely able to pay attention just to stand around the club the night before. So I decided Happy Hour on a Friday was the right choice.

I know some of my readers may be wondering, *"If you loved and cared about your friends, why go to the extent of just cutting people off?"* In the hall, I read the Bible a lot and Mark 10:29-30 tells us: "No one has left the house or family for my sake and for the sake of the good news who will not get 100 times more now....and in the coming system of things, everlasting life" *(New World Translation of the Holy Scriptures)*. I left my friends and my old ways for the reward of everlasting life in the future and for the new friends I'd gain.

Jesus prayed regarding his followers: "Sanctify them by means of the truth; your word is truth," John 17:17 *(New World Translation of the Holy Scriptures)*. "Sanctify them" can also mean "set them apart." I was taught that when we accept the truth and become true followers of Christ, we are set apart from the world because we no longer fit into its mold. I was taught I would be viewed differently because my values had changed. I was making a conscious choice to live by the standards of the Bible's truth. This was what I felt to be true.

I even canceled going to Miami Carnival AFTER I had already brought my costume and booked the accommodations, simply because I didn't want to put myself in a situation where I'd have to ask Jehovah to forgive me for my actions. I love carnival, but being half-naked in my carnival costume, drunk, and gyrating on every sexy man and woman within five feet of me seemed potentially problematic and not in line with my newfound beliefs. It was better for me to avoid it altogether–clubs, sex, partying–all of it.

I was happily single. I had even attained the highest possible achievement of my lifetime, celibacy. I had been a bisexual 20-something who loved to have sex with men and women, who was NEVER truly single and always dating. Achieving celibacy was an extreme accomplishment. I felt I had changed for the better. and I wasn't going to let the desires of my flesh and human imperfection mess that up for me. I had found self-control.

And yet, I decided to meet up with my old friend. I pulled up to 451 Lounge around 5 p.m. excited to have fun and fill her in and really enjoy the night. I gave her the longest embrace the moment I saw her. We smiled at each other as she grabbed my hand, and we giddily walked across the dance floor to our table. We sat down, ordered two drinks at half price, and unloaded all the information that we had missed over the last year.

I was at a pivotal place in my life and was so proud to share that with her. I had maintained my celibacy. I attended the Kingdom Hall faithfully and was well on the road to baptism. I stopped cursing. I drank only on special occasions, and I was very focused on my spiritual and mental growth. A lot had changed, and I was happy. I felt grounded. Just a year prior, my life was vastly different. I felt that I was changing for the better and the road to righteousness that I was on gave me clarity and personal peace that I hadn't experienced before.

It brought me joy to see a smile spread across her face as I shared my journey with her. I felt less guilty about leaving her out of my newfound life. She seemed proud of me and acknowledged our differences, and we agreed to find a way to remain friends regardless of all the changes.

We continued to share stories throughout the night and before you know it, we were three or four drinks in, which at the time was a lot for me considering I had basically stopped drinking. Truth be told, I was super tipsy at that point, which was probably the appropriate time to start making my exit, but I was having so much fun!!!! I hadn't had fun with my friend in so long and when 6 o'clock turned to 10 o'clock, I just kept rolling with it. I really wanted to just enjoy the night! So off to bar number two we went.

We got in my car and drove about two minutes down the road to the next spot. As we pulled up, I could hear the rhythmic beat of reggae music bellowing from the windows. We walked into the smoke-filled bar area, ordered our favorite cocktail, Rum Punch, and the night took off. A seedy drunken night that involved dancehall music, an ultraviolet light, and too many Rum Punches to count.

By the time we left the bar, it had to be after 1 a.m. and I was drunk as a skunk. So drunk that I literally felt weak. I remember driving back to her place, and I should not have been driving. I definitely should not have been drinking heavily, but there was no use crying over spilled milk, especially after I'd safely and miraculously pulled into the driveway.

There was absolutely no way I would've made it to my home a whopping 23 minutes away. We decided it would be best if I stayed the night. I was a burp away from vomit and two steps away from passing out, so it seemed like a solid decision. We stumbled in the door, laughing and recalling our night. She called her boyfriend and told me he'd be visiting for a nightcap as I sloppily found my way to her room and slumped down onto the bed. I changed into a t-shirt, kissed her goodnight, and rolled over to my respective side of the bed to retire into the deepest drunken stupor known to man. I was OUT!

It seemed like hours later when I began dreaming. I dreamt of hands touching every inch of me. Fingers running along my back and legs, kisses wet against my neck as I lay on my stomach immobile from intoxication. And then, I heard my name. My real name, (Britt -Tane -Knee), and for some reason, although I was dead to the world, hearing my name in my dream struck me as odd and awakened my senses. Where was the voice coming from? *"Who is that? Am I even dreaming at all? I must be,"* I thought, still in my drunken haze. I lay in my dream in her bed and began to drift off. As I drifted, the kissing on my neck continued as another hand found its way underneath my T-shirt and unhooked my bra.

I continued to lay flat on my stomach unable to recognize what exactly I was experiencing. The touching didn't cease, and my coherency didn't increase. I felt my underwear slide down past my knees and I began to hear voices again. Only these voices weren't inside my head. They seemed to be outside my head, speaking slowly, faintly. almost whispering. Someone was calling my name.

"Brittainy, can I?" the voice asked me repeatedly.

As hands caressed my neck I moaned, unable to speak. I felt a shift in my weight and a sharp stab and burning between my legs. Now I could feel everything. Every motion as I was painfully penetrated. He was inside of me while she rubbed my back and kissed my neck. I lay there in shock, unable to move as he violated every fiber of my being with her assistance. I groaned, unable to speak or wriggle free from their grasp. Soon, he finished and they both left the room. I continued to lay there shocked, in pain, and uncertain if it had even happened at all. I woke up in bed a few hours later and she lay soundly asleep at my side. I watched her sleep peacefully as I stealthily gathered as much of my things as I could find and ran out of there.

I never went to the police because at the time of the incident, her daughter was about six years old. I loved her more than her mother and in no way did I want to damage their relationship. I suffered in silence for a long time. A few months later, a mutual friend of ours encouraged me to talk to her about it and I did. I tried. I went back to that house and fought back tears as I began to relive every moment. We sat on her living room couch. I told her how much she hurt me. Her response was, *"I'm trying to be a better person now. What do you want me to do about it?"* That was the last time we spoke.

I tried to find some respite in returning to the hall. I tried turning to GOD to help me deal with the pain I suffered, the feeling of loss and agency of my own body. But when I turned to the elders (similar to a pastor), I found their advice only inflicted more pain and guilt as if what happened to me was my fault. I was basically told that if I hadn't placed myself in that situation, I wouldn't have suffered. I was even told that because of my sins, the drinking, and the unwanted sex, I was denying myself and my son the promise of everlasting life.

This information was relayed to me by a group of older men, as if they could ever understand what it feels like as a woman to be violated not only by a man but violated by two people at once. Raped at the hands of a friend. Without a doubt, their "counsel" is what pushed me out of the hall. There was one elder brother, and I truly wish I could remember his name, who I knew in my heart wanted to console me in a different way. Due to the hierarchy, he was not in charge of the conversation but when I told them what happened, he empathized and he cried with me.

All I needed was empathy and understanding, but I was denied that. I no longer felt safe or accepted so I left. I've visited the hall here and there since, but nothing even remotely close to before. I do not judge those who identify as Witnesses, but my experience was tarnished. I've still retained a lot of my Bible teachings and Jehovah remains in my heart, but I no longer feel the same about the Kingdom Hall.

To my attackers.

You know who you are. I was quiet then, but I refuse to be silent now. Part of the reason I never spoke up is because I was in shock. I couldn't comprehend what happened to me at the hands of someone who

I considered a friend. Someone who I trusted, who knew I was celibate and that I had changed my lifestyle. I didn't understand how you could do that to me after I told you about all the changes I made in my life. I was happy and you intentionally tried to take that from me.

The other reason for my silence came from pure sympathy for you and your daughter. As someone who has dealt with joint custody since my son was two-and-a-half years old, in no way did I want to impact the relationship between you and your daughter. In no way did I want her to lose any time with her mom. No matter how fucked up the situation was, I still considered you and your child. I still managed to put love first.

What you both did that night was detestable. I was incoherent and taken advantage of. Both of you raped me. Ephesians 4:32 tells us: "Be kind and compassionate to one another, freely forgiving one another as GOD through Christ freely forgave you." I have not mastered the art of forgiveness but I tried. I tried to forgive you. I tried giving you the opportunity to make amends, but there was no accountability. There was no sincerity, no remorse, no regard for how your actions impacted me. So instead of forgiving and forgetting, I've chosen to simply let go. Let go of the pain inflicted on me. Let go of the shame I once harbored for myself due to what I experienced that night. Let go of the fear placed in my heart.

Instead, I have found courage. Courage means finding something more important than fear. I found my voice. I've spoken my truth about something I tried to bury inside of me that plagued my heart for years.

I sincerely hope that both of you have worked on yourselves and have become better individuals, if not for you then for your children, the people around you, the people in your life who look up to you. What legacy are you leaving in the world for those people? What legacy are you leaving behind for yourselves?

I wish no ill will toward either of you. I've forgiven myself for the blame I placed on my own spirit and come to realize that you cannot control the actions of others. I hope you both find peace, courage, and forgiveness.

Brittainy

REALITY CHECK:

My aunt taught me to never give anyone your power. Throughout the course of my life, I lost my power and sight of myself many times and in many ways. Yet, in losing ourselves, I have found that there is always a dimly lit path inside of us to help find our way back. I want you to think about different ways in which you can give power back to yourself when you feel lost. How will you find your own way to heal or cope when the going gets tough? I want you to know that using your voice to help yourself or someone else is exercising your own power. I encourage you to use your voice and know that you are powerful. Dealing with past trauma is not easy. I doubt it will ever be, but taking the time to try and learn from the past, to try to heal can impact your future self in powerful ways. I myself am still learning, growing, and healing. Each day is different. Life is a journey and you have the power to embark on your journey and change the course at any time. You are in control of how dim or bright the light within you shines. What will you do when your light starts to become dim? Feel free to journal below.

_____

_____

_____

_____

_____

_____

_____

_____

_____

_____

_____

_____

_____

_____

_____

ONE LAST WORD

KNOW AT MOMENTS this was a tough read, and I thank you for making it to the end with me. Let's decompress our emotions and pause for a minute to take a couple of deep breaths. In through your nose and out through your mouth. One more time. In through your nose and out through your mouth.

I want you to know I am okay. I've learned to forgive myself for the mistakes I've made. I've learned to let go of the pain caused by others and for the mistakes of their younger, unhealed selves. I'm grateful for the lessons I've learned. A good therapist has been a godsend for me, and I attend therapy every single week. That does not mean every day is easy or that I've mastered life, but I do have the support that I need to help me get through difficult moments.

In addition to therapy, I try to practice self-care daily. I like to practice yoga or listen to meditation music throughout my work day or some other form of loving on myself. Sometimes I meditate, I read, I even have affirmations posted to my mirror that I try to recite when I'm feeling doubtful, or I listen to affirmations on YouTube. When all of those things don't seem to work, I pray. I ask my Creator to wrap me in love and comfort me. I do not seek the pity of any of my readers, I only ask for your recognition that I am here, standing on my own two feet and using the power of my voice to speak out.

Thank you for riding this emotional rollercoaster with me. I'm sure some of my readers, specifically those who know me personally, might be in shock or surprised. Those who don't know me are likely to have a similar reaction. Truth is, I chose to write this memoir to help me heal, to let go of some of the emotional things in my life that I gave too much power to, and to help others find their voice.

This memoir is an act of self-love, a way to release everything! It is an act of bravery and courage as I use my voice and own my power! Far too often we lose our voices in this world for many reasons. I'm done being quiet. I'm done making myself small to appease others or fit in. I am uniquely me and my experiences have contributed to who I am. I am proud to have overcome a lot of shit. There's still plenty of shit to get through because that's how life is. It's not always easy.

If anyone reading this has experienced similar or worse situations, I'm here to affirm that you can get through it too. But I encourage you not to try doing it alone. Use whatever resources you have and find outlets. My outlets are writing and therapy. Find what works for you and then find a way to release whatever feelings, pain, or experiences no longer serve you.

At first, I wasn't sure how my experience(s) had anything at all to do with the woman I've become and continue to grow into. Then it hit me. I am a Diversity Equity and Inclusion (DEI) program manager. The main reason I pursued my role was because I felt the voices of marginalized groups were being stifled at work. I saw missed opportunities and a lot of unfair treatment. Luckily, I have an amazing CEO who expressed plainly to our Black Indigenous People of Color (BIPOC) communities in the workplace, *"If you see something that is unfair, tell me."* I took that opportunity and wrote my CEO a letter in which I truthfully expressed to her my experiences, and the experiences of my friends who had either been terminated or left the company. I detailed other things I was seeing that were unfair, unjust, and did not align with the company's goals. Making the decision to use my voice in that moment propelled my future and jump-started my career in DEI. Of course people complained, but there's a huge difference between complaining and actually doing something about it. I decided to do something about it and less than a year later, my career began.

The work I do is vital. I know what it feels like to be bullied, misunderstood, and unrepresented. I know what it's like to feel invisible and that you don't belong. In my role, I am part of the solution to making sure everyone feels like they belong. I help make sure people are treated fairly and their voices are heard. I am part of that change. I want each of you to know there is power in your voice and power in speaking up. This is my first book, but it is certainly not my last. I will continue to *SPEAK*, and you must as well.

ABOUT THE AUTHOR

BRITTAINY SPENCER BEGAN writing her memoir as early as 2019 before putting the pedal to the metal in 2021 and committing to sharing her truth. She is a proud mother and leader in Diversity Equity and Inclusion. Passionate about love, justice, and fairness, she has used her experiences to fuel her career to support marginalized communities. Brittainy currently resides in Connecticut with her son, London.

Looking to connect with Brittainy? You can find her on LinkedIn.

LinkedIn (67) Brittainy Spencer | LinkedIn.

Printed in the USA
CPSIA information can be obtained
at www.ICGtesting.com
LVHW012051241123
764800LV00011B/671